I Won't Apologize For Being a Woman
SPECIAL EDITION

By
Zorina Exie Jerome
© 2010

Featuring

new poems and

a bonus chapter of Zorina Exie Jerome's next book
How to Conquer Haters

I Won't Apologize For Being a Woman SPECIAL EDITION
by Zorina Exie Jerome

I Won't Apologize For Being a Woman, Special Edition
ISBN 9-781456-336561
Copyright © 2010

How to Conquer Haters
Copyright © 2010

An
I.W.A.
project.
© Copyright 2010

Library of Congress in Publication Data
Jerome, Zorina Exie
Little Girl, Walk with Me / Zorina Exie Jerome
Copyright © September 1997
I Won't Apologize For Being a Woman / Zorina Exie Jerome
Copyright © 2006
by Zorina Exie Jerome

Photo by Katie Fairfield-Krieder

All rights reserved.

No part of this book may be reproduced or transmitted in any form or by any means, electronic or mechanical, including photocopying, recording, or by any information storage and retrieval system without written consent of the author except where permitted by law.

I Won't Apologize For Being a Woman SPECIAL EDITION
by Zorina Exie Jerome

In Loving Memory of Margaret Ann

I Won't Apologize For Being a Woman
SPECIAL EDITION
By
Zorina Exie Jerome
© 2010

Featuring

new poems and

a bonus chapter of Zorina Exie Jerome's next book

How to Conquer Haters

I Won't Apologize For Being a Woman SPECIAL EDITION
by Zorina Exie Jerome

CONTENTS

Your Sister	7
Order	9
Tick-Tock	10
Issues	12
So Sexy	13
Trust or Lust?	15
Diggin'	17
Letting You Know	19
Mascarade	21
Break up or Make up?	22
A Woman of Worth	24
He Sleeps	27
Awaken	30
This Is Me	33
Hating: Independent Decisions	35
Chickenhead	37
You've Got to Love Yourself	39
Spiritual Creeping: CHEATING	41
Testimony	43
Not Feeling It	47
Compromise	50
Denial	52
Not Having It	53
You Can Love Again	54
Write Off	55
Oh Yes. Sexy Dress.	56

I Won't Apologize For Being a Woman SPECIAL EDITION
by Zorina Exie Jerome

    Cordial   58
    What's Her Purpose?   63
    *It's a Weave. Get Over It!   66

BONUS CHAPTER
How to Conquer Haters
    Chapter 1: What is a Hater?   70

I Won't Apologize For Being a Woman SPECIAL EDITION
by Zorina Exie Jerome

YOUR SISTER

What's up?

How have you been?

I can tell you have been through a lot. You may not know me very well but, I can tell because

I'm your sister.

You may think I don't understand. That I cannot comprehend God's plan for you.

True! Because nobody can understand you but The Almighty. Feisty becomes your attitude when you get in the mood where you need to meditate. So, I leave you to pray and make no mistake, I'll show my love because

I'm your sister.

I may not understand your business sense or your personal life but I understand your appetite for The Spirit. God bless you and your generation seven times down if creation is still in exist, if God permits. I say this in the name of The Father, The Son, and The Holy Spirit. I'm trying to forget what is materialistic. Trying to get ready for The Kingdom made of gold.

The one where all new things are made from old, aren't you ready to go?

You may not know me but I'll tell you this: my faith may be the size of a mustard seed. Yet, I see some of what you see and you see some of what I see.

Don't you know we're trying to form Christ as a whole? Trying to testify how we gained our might in these last days. We're coming together like crusades.

Trying to warn our mothers and fathers to prepare their sons and daughters for that great meteor shower along with the moans and hollers.

Drug dealers are still trying to make a dollar and they might burn in the lake of fire.

I Won't Apologize For Being a Woman SPECIAL EDITION
by Zorina Exie Jerome

You may think I'm too young to understand but, I know of God's unchanging hand.

Share with me what I don't see then I'll share with you what is in me.

Get used to me.

We'll be together for eternity.

Along with The Holy Father and him and her because,

I am

your sister.

I Won't Apologize For Being a Woman SPECIAL EDITION
by Zorina Exie Jerome

ORDER

Coming to the revelation I've entered a new realm of life,
I might as well fall on my knees and pray...

Young mothers constantly sliding off their panties so they can find their baby a new daddy because daddy found a new home to play house in.

With a little momma not knowing.

Follow me now:

As long as he's sexing her right, sleeps over every night, everything's alright. Meanwhile, his baby is in the arms of another man who has a plan to buy the child diapers and milk from the can.

While he's at it, some condoms. Pick a brand, any brand. He knew her baby's father. He wasn't having that at all.

All the while, his new play-wife is scratching his car with a knife because his baby's mother dialed a *69.

This is a cycle we might all get caught in if we fall in love too quick, mistaking a prick or a trick as a quick fix but, I'm here to tell you this:

It all can be avoided once we choose to set our priorities straight.

Meditate as well as communicate with the next generation who holds our fate.

Remember when Eve took the fruit from the tree? Taking what she didn't need.

Are we repeating history? Could this be?

A brother jealous of another? Over what? The other lover?

Whatever.

In the meantime, let's keep our brains sane and stop playing games.

I Won't Apologize For Being a Woman SPECIAL EDITION
by Zorina Exie Jerome

TICK-TOCK

Wait. Wait. Wait.
That's all I seem to do while time
is ticking.
Tick-Tock.
Tick-Tock.
I look in the mirror.
Dang.
Time has stopped
for me. I see youth
renewed in me.
More energy. More beauty.
I love me.
If I'm going to wait,
It might as well be with somebody like me.
Who likes me.
Who likes their reflection
and can say,
"I love me."
"I love you."
Now that's me.
That's what I like.
That's how to be.
That's how to love me.
Now time has been ticking.
Ticking.
While I've been thinking.

I Won't Apologize For Being a Woman SPECIAL EDITION
by Zorina Exie Jerome

Ticking while I've been waiting.

Ticking while I've been praying.

Ticking.

Tick-Tock.

Look now.

The clock stopped.

I Won't Apologize For Being a Woman SPECIAL EDITION
by Zorina Exie Jerome

ISSUES

I remember when I first noticed you.

So dark. So tall. Dare I stare?

Didn't want you to notice me notice you.
Didn't want anyone to know I cared.

I remember when we first met.

Everywhere I went, you were already there.
With no plans, no particular time set.
It just seemed natural to have you near.

I remember our first date.
It was too smooth. Too good to be true.

I allowed circumstances to rise. To intimidate.
To create and elevate more issues.

What is exactly wrong with believing what's good is true?
Why do we allow our joy to be extinguished by issues?

I Won't Apologize For Being a Woman SPECIAL EDITION
by Zorina Exie Jerome

SO SEXY

Excuse me.

I know I'm saved and
I'm really not trying to run any game but

Why are you so sexy to me?

I mean, you look really good to me!

I look at you and my thoughts get misconstrued you
shouldn't be allowed to walk around in those tight shirts.

Whose feelings are you trying to hurt?

Now, I know I'm saved and supposed to be setting an example.
But I'd be lying to myself if I said I didn't want a sample!

I'm just being real.
How many sisters out there can feel what I'm stressing?

Might as well expose it.
Before my flesh tries to show it.
And folks blow it,
all out of proportion.

I am still being kept by God's grace.

I Won't Apologize For Being a Woman SPECIAL EDITION
by Zorina Exie Jerome

Except

my mind sometimes struggles

of thoughts of those muscles

that can get me in trouble

if I don't buckle my knees on the double.

Thoughts are subtle

from the view I see.

May I ask you again,

Why are you so sexy?

The way you strut isn't even funny.
Got me truly pleading, "Lord have mercy on me!"

He's the one who made you sexy.

I Won't Apologize For Being a Woman SPECIAL EDITION
by Zorina Exie Jerome

TRUST OR LUST?

So you want to know if you can trust me?
Yeah Babe, I can read that question right off your face.
Trying to hide it with a transparent look,
thinking there's no trace.

Well to tell you the truth, I really don't know.
I'll be the first to admit,
in almost every woman,
there is a little whore.

Oh no?!
Don't act surprised.

I saw your girlfriend eyeing another guy while
you were giving me the eye. I
cannot help but to do what is in my nature.
Eve made it tough for us. For that,
childbirth is tough but,
if you want to know if you can trust me,
then you'll have to let that lust decease and
take time out to know the real me.

I wear my heart on my sleeve.
Trouble is, selfish ones crush it and
make it bleed.

I Won't Apologize For Being a Woman SPECIAL EDITION
by Zorina Exie Jerome

Once the blood is gone,

it can never come back.

For that reason, in relationships you may think

I don't know how to act.

Like what?

How your ex-girlfriend used to?

Aw Boo.

Can

I

trust

you?

I Won't Apologize For Being a Woman SPECIAL EDITION
by Zorina Exie Jerome

DIGGIN'

I dig you.

Whatever you have to do,

cool.

I would like to hear from you, see about you, talk to you but if I don't,

Cool.

I'll be me and you be you.

Do what you need to do.

Who knows?

I just might be waiting for you.

I dig you. I'm

breaking my rules. I'm

playing it cool. I'm

doing what I need to do to get through.

I oftentimes think about you. No feelings involved, so I'm alright. Emotions tight.

Looking to the light. Fighting this good fight. Getting through the nights.

Brave like a knight.

You don't have to call.

I will be alright.

No hard feelings. Not taking it personal.

Nevermind.

You get yours and I'll get mine. Not trying to rewind time.

I'm diggin'

I Won't Apologize For Being a Woman SPECIAL EDITION
by Zorina Exie Jerome

a foundation for the next generation of priestly nations the invitation is still open.

I will keep hoping, serving, believing, receiving, praising, raising my hands in surrender.

I'm diggin' so when a storm appears, my household will not fear.

I'm diggin' so when it's time to arise, I'll stay grounded. Not aroused by irrelevant knowledge.

Conquered that in college.

I'm diggin'

so when my children come, they will have some of

the inheritance.

They'll learn to give the excess.

It only causes stress. It's best to let it rest.

I'm diggin'.

You

better believe that.

I'm diggin'.

I Won't Apologize For Being a Woman SPECIAL EDITION
by Zorina Exie Jerome

LETTING YOU KNOW

Whatever you heard about me,
believe that.
How I used to trip?
It was like that.
Now tell me,
what do you think about that?
My love is never bad.
Never getting none of that unless it's meant to be
sealed with a kiss and a wedding ring.
Everything you might have heard
regarding attitude was all true. So,
now what do you want to do?

Be real with me and I'll give you some time.
Tell me your weakness and I'll tell you mine. I'll cover up yours and you
cover up mine.
Rearrange my schedule.

Trying to make this possible. With you, it might be worth a shot, so why not?

Not sacrificing anything yet, still contemplating. Still waiting. Debating if you are for real. Keeping my guard up. I'm just being real.
Anxious to inspect your fruit but, not the nectar. Not trying to play that.

I Won't Apologize For Being a Woman SPECIAL EDITION
by Zorina Exie Jerome

I know better.

So whatever you heard about me is probably true. Know I've grown in the things of The Lord. What do you want to do?

Hated and humiliated.

Chastened daily.

Fighting everything that is not of God.

Even my mind.

Do you really want to tangle with this mind?

If so let's go tango. It will be difficult to let you lead but, I've been trained to let a man be. . . a man.

Really, I still don't fully understand. So take my hand

and guide me slowly.

Remain among the meek and lowly. You know me. Christ in

me but you don't know what He's done to me, in me, through me

Constantly.

Allow me to introduce me.

I am who I'm supposed to be.

So don't try to change me. Pray for me.

Remember that.

I Won't Apologize For Being a Woman SPECIAL EDITION
by Zorina Exie Jerome

MASCARADE

You wished and you wished for me.
Prayed to God for Him to send
me to you.
Now that you have me,
you don't know what to do.
How many times did you wish
to have a companion like yourself?
Recognize.
The same qualities you can't stand about me,
are the very same ones that attracted you to me.

I Won't Apologize For Being a Woman SPECIAL EDITION
by Zorina Exie Jerome

BREAK UP OR MAKE-UP?

I had to let you know.
Now I have to let this thing go.
I can't allow myself to be hindered.
I must be free to be me.
To come forth is like a dying seed.
Father, help me, I don't really know what
that means.
Feelings of energy released inside me.
Hunger subdued. Something new
inside me.

To give something good and then
take it away from me
is like planting a deep kiss on my lips in the midst
of this interlude that doesn't want to be over.

Dang!

It feels like I found a four-leaf clover.
But
Could it just be my need to have a man walk next to me?
Could it just be my own thoughts of what I think it should be?
Could it just be me catching him instead of him catching me?
Could it just be me needing to grow up, beating
myself up
for no reason?

I Won't Apologize For Being a Woman SPECIAL EDITION
by Zorina Exie Jerome

Is it just me blaming the demon for my own demented reasoning?

I've got to let this thing go!

I just wanted to let you know, that
If you can put up with me,
you will definitely share
the blessings
purposed for me.

I Won't Apologize For Being a Woman SPECIAL EDITION
by Zorina Exie Jerome

A WOMAN OF WORTH

Who can find a virtuous woman?
Her worth is far above silver.
For when the fire comes, worldly treasures will wither.

To live virtuously is to stand God's ground.
No matter how it looks,
no matter how it sounds.

Our inheritance is good.
Ready to produce abundant fruit at the set time. Versatile is the sower.
Ruler of all kind.

Some soil is labored on.
Some soil is producing.
Some soil is kept.
Some women allow their soil to get trampled and spoiled on, while Saints pray on to keep strong.

Waiting.

Patiently waiting while God gives the increase.
Keeping our land pure while men sought land with grass which grew too quickly.

Kneeling, they found the grass was indeed weed.

I Won't Apologize For Being a Woman SPECIAL EDITION
by Zorina Exie Jerome

While the virtuous woman's seed pleases The Father who feeds the seed, enriched in all things.

Who can find, a virtuous woman?

Her worth is far above money.

More precious than gold.

Sweeter than honey.

Because she deceased from being in Eve. Take heed!

The Holy Ghost pleads your case in case you didn't know.

Jesus claimed you innocent. White as snow as long as you know who you are.

You don't have to act like a superstar just so someone can acknowledge who you are.

In God is where you are.

Your submission to His will shall prove you to be strong by the act of your own faith. It will increase your success by far.

Who can find a virtuous woman? Her worth is far above prestige. Isn't too proud to be and rejoices in Christ who set her free.

She will try to resist the spirit of lust because her God is with her as a mighty and terrible one, who gave His only begotten son to lay down his life for lost ones and resurrected the third day for the justification of everyone.

I Won't Apologize For Being a Woman SPECIAL EDITION
by Zorina Exie Jerome

Respect your body of The Holy One.

Refrain from speaking an unholy tongue.

Women need to stand and represent what God is all about or sit there trying to be cute,

choosing to be a jewel in a swine's snout.

It is said that charm is deceitful and beauty is vain but

a woman who fears The Lord,

will have blessed days.

I Won't Apologize For Being a Woman SPECIAL EDITION
by Zorina Exie Jerome

HE SLEEPS

No need to wake him.

He sleeps.

Look at him. Even as he sleeps, he is confident. Strong in The Lord, is He.

Firmly standing as

He sleeps.

Longing for him to notice me. Wanting the longing to cease as

He sleeps.

Wanting him does me no good when the wanting is when I want it under my own conditions. Not to mention he's not even moved when I make my move.

Knowing that it's You in me who moves. Yet, his eyes

won't even flutter.

He sleeps.

With his eyes closed, how could he recognize me? I need to know he loves me.

Why won't he direct his attention toward me?

"Hey you, over there, look at me! Everyone else does, so why can't you see Christ in me?" Father embraces his calmness about me and whispers,

"He sleeps."

I Won't Apologize For Being a Woman SPECIAL EDITION
by Zorina Exie Jerome

God, will you please wake him up?

I reach to wake him with a loving touch. The same place I touch is the same place I came from.

His tender side, I find.

Subconsciously, he doesn't like that I am able to find the vulnerable spot he thought only our Father knew about but God has allowed me to touch him there too, for it was I who came from that womb.

His first reaction was as loving as love. Then he realizes I am just like him.

He squeezed his eyes tight, jerked away from me and mumbled,

"Leave me alone. I'm asleep."

Oh my! He thinks I'm an angel in disguise. Was I? Trying to jump ahead of things by doing my own thing? I heard many voices saying:

Leave him with me. Like you, I'm working on him as

He sleeps.

For once, take your eyes away from him. Look up and around you. Enjoy the fruits. There are some things you are ordained to tend to.

Reluctantly, I rose from his side.

I Won't Apologize For Being a Woman SPECIAL EDITION
by Zorina Exie Jerome

Daddy is calling now. Continue to rest. I believe you'll be all right. I'll be waiting for you when you awake. For now, there are some things our Father wants me to say.

So I kissed him with the breath of my words.

And off I went to tend to the herbs.

I Won't Apologize For Being a Woman SPECIAL EDITION
by Zorina Exie Jerome

AWAKEN

She became so in tuned with her work to please her Father. Knowing He would bless her and when man awoke, she'd share with him all that she earned. Her motivation was to please her Father first. The love he reigned over her was as potent as precipitation.

She wanted for nothing.

Yes, she was one of his many favorites. So she savored this.

And the weight of His glory, she wore.

She shined a majestic splendor reflected from El Shaddai, having great confidence in Him, she'd never die.

Suddenly Envy, Jealously, and Slander crept by her side. They tried to enter man but his armor was on too tight. Plus, he was in a holy rest. In the fortress. In His breast.

So Envy, Jealousy and Slander surrounded her. Disguised as an angel of light to betray her. Envy, Jealously, and Slander scurried about her. Like little foxes attempting to spoil her herbs.

If these Spirits were here before her, no wonder man was so stern towards her. She attempted to approach him to declare,

"No, I'm not like them."

I Won't Apologize For Being a Woman SPECIAL EDITION
by Zorina Exie Jerome

By then, the foxes had stolen enough virtue to look and act somewhat like her. The alleged angel of light glared a stare of hate. Still smiling though saying,

"He's not worth the wait."

Suddenly, appears the spirit of Hate. Consuming Jealously, Envy, and Slander, transforming itself into one big snake.

It suggests, "Taste and see that I am sweet. I will give you all the attention you need. Let him lay there ignoring you as he sleeps. For I never sleep so let me plant my seed."

These are the very words she wanted to hear from her man. Unmistakable confirmation that he too can understand.

Although this snake appeared to have it going on, there was still a place in her he couldn't touch on. It was the core of her existence which came from man. The origin of man's rib that God built as woman. It was the divine place within her where The Father and her man can coincide. The snake tried, yet she wasn't feeling that vibe. So she sighed and looked over to her sleeping mate.

She thinks *I can see why he still sleeps. For I fellowship with his enemies, Slander, Jealousy and Envy.*

"Father forgive me," She pleads. "For, I allowed myself to be distracted. I'm no longer ignorant to this device. Lord, I

I Won't Apologize For Being a Woman SPECIAL EDITION
by Zorina Exie Jerome

know you have my back. So I'm going to let your light shine in how I act.

So she looks back at the snake and says, "Not today. Not ever. In any way. I have a more important task for the day. Like warning the world about your wicked ways. I'm going to warn my man him about JeZebel, Delilah. . ."

"Don't forget Eve too," her man chimed. "I remember how in the Garden of Eden, you deceived her but this here is my woman, whom I prayed to Jehovah-Jireh for, to be wise and rightly able to discern. This is my bride, my love, my treasure and warrior. We command you to flee and never return! My God opened my eyes to witness the faithfulness of my bride. Although she was tried, her love for me never died."

For only a short time he was asleep. Though, it may have seemed long. From then on, their ministry carried on to their descendants and to the faithful ones who were once illegitimate.

I Won't Apologize For Being a Woman SPECIAL EDITION
by Zorina Exie Jerome

THIS IS ME

Why are you scared of me?
Do you think if I see the real you,
you'd see me flee?
Who's to say I wouldn't and who's to say I would?
Who's to say if you're not disturbed every time I enter a room,
you don't care? And
Who's to say if my very presence adds another beat to your heaven,
I don't become moved? We
move
Things. We
effect things. We
got this thing going on, but I can't seem to put my finger on it.
It's like it moves the minute I pursue it and
my hand glides the pen to find it to
search for the answer. Even God
won't give me the full answer and umm,
I feel left out, man! Oftentimes, a little bummed out. Sometimes
the pressure becomes too much and
I want out!
But I've already seen the real thing. So
I test it to prove that it's the real thing. I'm
going to continue to because
I am scared of you.
You
have this thing in you that moves

I Won't Apologize For Being a Woman SPECIAL EDITION
by Zorina Exie Jerome

this thing in me I can't control and

that scares me.

I'm not sure if I know what that means. You

inspire me.

I don't even like you!

You have this thing about you that moves me to believe

we are supposed to be

together?

I'm not sure.

Confused.

I'm scared of you.

There.

I said it.

I don't know what else to do.

I Won't Apologize For Being a Woman SPECIAL EDITION
by Zorina Exie Jerome

HATING: INDEPENDENT DECISIONS

Bought for a price.

That's how you got your wife.

Now you must spend your life

with she who manipulated and contemplated how she would keep you from making your own choice.

Covering your mouth from using your own voice.

Redeeming you like a UPC symbol. Cashing you in like some money-hungry bimbo.

It's hard not think about it, when everyone seems to talk about it.

Trying hard not to act phony. But, you say it's all about the money. Honey-Child, please!

See.

Those riches can go as easy as they came. It doesn't have anything to do with game.

Everything belongs to The Lord who gives as He sees fit because He bought us for a price with his life.

You choose not to believe, which is why you are easily persuaded with money.

She knows this.

So she holds this over your head.

Possessed with Delilah.

She's going to wear you down

until you are tired.

Cut your strength off something crafty-like.

Now your blind.

But there is still time to call on The Lord who already bought you with the

price of His life.

I Won't Apologize For Being a Woman SPECIAL EDITION
by Zorina Exie Jerome

Ask Him to rescue you from the life you thought was going to be gravy.

Give it all up for the sake of sanity.

Then you'll truly see what real happiness means.

More precious than silver.

Worth more than gold.

He has the power to redeem new things from old.

Bought with a price.

Open your mouth.

Use your voice.

Speak and make

your own choice.

I Won't Apologize For Being a Woman SPECIAL EDITION
by Zorina Exie Jerome

CHICKENHEAD

Chickenhead, chickenhead.

How can I tell you, you've been misled? Thinking you're all that because of the zeros in your checkbook. Look again and see that it all amounts up to zero.

Do you think you have a hero? What are you going to do when the devil draws his bow back to attack? In your eyes, I lack. No, you didn't say it but you did in how you act.

As a matter of fact will your hero protect you? Will he speak life into your situation or will he tear you down with evil sayings? Oh, you think I'm hating? I stopped playing a long time ago. Didn't care anymore to wear the title of a "Ho" so, I roll on. Hating the games silly women play. Make no mistake, I had my day. That's why I'm able to call your play a mile away and that's what I hate.

I hate you pick flowers before they have had a chance to bloom. I hate how you think you are superior anytime you walk into a room. I hate my envy over your fruits but because you picked too soon, I know your fruit must be bittersweet.

It really doesn't look that way to me.

See, only what you do for Christ will last. I've got to remind myself of that every time you want to style and flash, Chickenhead!

I Won't Apologize For Being a Woman SPECIAL EDITION
by Zorina Exie Jerome

Chickenhead, chickenhead! How I wish I could tell you, you've been misled. Even though it looks like you have everything right, I know something isn't right! Right now, I'm going to keep my mouth shut because the grace of God is everywhere. I've seen some Christians not care. Rising high like the Savior, then evaporating like vapor. Only if you're in His divine favor, will you get out of tight spots like Whodini. You seem to be perplexed because I spat a couple riddles!

If you past your tests, then waiting for you, is God's best. You think you've got the best? Well, wait until your hero sandwiches you in and sinks you like a sub because he had no substance of what's heaven-sent. Now you're wondering what I meant. This poem is not about me venting. It's about waiting and recognizing instead of hunting and gathering any man who will give you immediate attention. Instead of plucking this and that, perhaps it is simply time to sit and hatch an idea that involves self-improvement, positive solutions that include a spiritual movement which leaves you content with who you are to determine a new level of self-worth like a precious metal, something you would not exchange for just anything.

But alas,

Chickenheads will just go for anything.

I Won't Apologize For Being a Woman SPECIAL EDITION
by Zorina Exie Jerome

YOU'VE GOT TO LOVE YOURSELF

Before we can begin to love and accept one another, we need to love and accept ourselves. This is a common saying, faithful only in good deeds. Yet, how many of us are actually acting out on these things?

How can we accept common things when actually we run from our own being?

We pray the prayer of purging with supplication but when our true selves come out, we want to take a vacation! There's nothing wrong with that but keep an open mind! If we shut ourselves away from everyone and everything then how will lost ones know the true way once we go solo on our own journey?

Perhaps to spare them of our own self whom we can't stand to be around?

Remember God sent Jesus to lead the lost to the found. So with all of your getting, get the understanding that this is not a phase you're going through. It's a constant thing. To despise yourself is to despise someone else.

You've got to love yourself.

You have to love yourself.

You better love yourself.

If not then you're loving something else which really isn't love at all.

I Won't Apologize For Being a Woman SPECIAL EDITION
by Zorina Exie Jerome

It is lust and infatuation giving you a brief fix to your current crisis on a situation. You better listen!

God isn't playing!

If you just sit there acting like you don't care, like you don't love yourself, how can you help those who need help?

Patience?

Patience.

Patience is a virtue. Patience gets you ready for the blessings and responsibilities God has for you.

This may be taken as a rebuke for those whom this may only concern.

But really, this is also intended for the molding and shaping for those who are willing and ready to learn.

Frustration will distract your focus every time.

Do not become dissatisfied with yourself

Remember, you are who you are only because of God's grace and mercy.

I Won't Apologize For Being a Woman SPECIAL EDITION
by Zorina Exie Jerome

SPIRITUAL CREEPING: CHEATING

Avoiding superfluity of you and me between the sheets, I look past the heavenly boundaries that separate me from what is unknown. It does not make sense for me to stress what is already done.

You're on your own to find your way home.

Apostle Paul said it is better not to marry but if I can't control myself, marry.

I remain merry because The Savior, in me, I tarry.

Barely making it on my own. Enemies come and enemies go. Which is why the breastplate of righteousness guards my soul. Immune to false teaching. My helmet of salvation, I'm reaching. Stepping over enemies of iniquity because Jesus died and is made alive. I

recognize He is bigger than you and me.

We

can't outsmart the creator of Heaven and Earth.

Omnipotent he be's.
Magnificent are His deeds.
Awesome are His works
all because He is Lord.

I Won't Apologize For Being a Woman SPECIAL EDITION
by Zorina Exie Jerome

So put that thing away.

Before we make a baby.

Stay away from me.

Until you get yourself together. Better

to marry,

than to burn with passion.

So The Bible says.

I Won't Apologize For Being a Woman SPECIAL EDITION
by Zorina Exie Jerome

TESTIMONY

No matter what we do, it's judged on judgment day. So kill those bitter feelings life in this strange life.

I was caught up in the mix. My man was tricking a trick who was looking for a quick fix to feed her kids. She had to get by, by any means necessary. Even if it meant to bogart strong, creating an adversary. Now I was an average girl nice and wholesome and all.

Listening to my daddy bang my mommy's head up against the wall. Looking at my sisters fall into a tangled web of men. Never could understand why they had to raise their hand.

At night I'd hear my sisters cry and wonder why can't I leave and flee this urban plight. I'll set my sights on any man who held a genuine interest in me. He'll intercede and treat me how my daddy should've treated me. I was looking for daddy and daddy was who I found except these little boys always tried to slide my pants down. This made me frown. A quick smile, again turned upside down.

No matter what we do, it's judged on judgment day. So kill those bitter feelings life in this strange life.

This strange life led me into the arms of a boy who had charm. He held a job at 16, working the restaurant scene. Little me was impressed so I suggest to open my chest to love him unconditionally. A true candidate to spoil me as his one and only. No kids or nothing. This sounds like a plan! I think I can keep this man!

"I love you, baby," He said to me.

And I knew we couldn't be defeated.

Pumps and bumps! Our pelvis's rubbed up! Exploring in different ways. My man, I'd lay. My sexuality, I wanted to play. For then his loyalty I knew I'd really win his best interest at heart. Never thought he'd play the game of darts with my heart.

As a young black man, he knew this world was shady. He looked at other ladies. He sometimes touched up. He knew he messed up when he brought to me that drug they called cream.

He said, "Baby, Look! See! I can sell this here and make a quick 20."

I said, "For real? Go out there and sell us more!"

Twenties turned into quarters. Quarters turned into kilos! I'm riding high in a souped-up ride sitting on chrome rims! My man was rolling! A kingpin! We knew we were sinning because he sold the cream and I reaped the benefits that was killing them, us...

That dust just didn't settle right with me because now I'm driving a get-a-way car and had a gun up to my brother's head because he tried to take my man's life from making all that bread.

I Won't Apologize For Being a Woman SPECIAL EDITION
by Zorina Exie Jerome

Now I eat the bread of Christ I try to be like and hold my head up with no shame. Not trying to live the lifestyle of rolling and cruising the coast of Jamaica, living the life of some crusader.

No matter what we do, it's judged on judgment day. So kill those bitter feelings life in this strange life.

It hurts to love, I found out in life. I spied on my guy. I knew he wasn't right. Females was calling and bugging, flexing and testing me all because they wanted to be me.

I couldn't see. Thought the world revolved around me. I wasn't trying to hear about Jesus.

Once I got my hands on that girl, there was definitely static as I let loose my 38 automatic.

I missed! I couldn't believe this!

Fiending for the sight of blood, I sought the blood of Christ.

Repenting from popping the pistol. Go and figure what Satan will have you do when you're caught up in the world, clowning like a fool. My heart was wounded.

Foolish, ghoulish angels manipulate, agitate, perpetrate and concentrate on their hate. Even their own fate, they try to control but Jesus, Emmanuel has that remote control.

I Won't Apologize For Being a Woman SPECIAL EDITION
by Zorina Exie Jerome

My plan foiled to live my life the way I thought was right. But like the Bible says, "We walk by faith and not by sight."

I try to be the light.

Don't forget, don't use your sight.

Let God fight your battles.

I Won't Apologize For Being a Woman SPECIAL EDITION
by Zorina Exie Jerome

NOT FEELING IT

My first date
was on a Wednesday.
Quite late.
Momma didn't know
she thought I went to a basketball game around eight.
Daddy didn't care.
He was too busy asking momma,
"Did you wash my underwear?"

Nobody cared.

But my new boyfriend did.
A 20-year-old high school drop-out claimed he could easily please
a girl like me
at the age of 16.

As long as he had money,
that's all I needed.

He called my school.
Said he was my father.
Said I couldn't make it.
Cough, flu, something or other.
Invited me over to his house
or should I say his momma's basement.
Wanted to talk.

I Won't Apologize For Being a Woman SPECIAL EDITION
by Zorina Exie Jerome

Thought he was gonna hit it.

"Nah, I can't make it. I don't have a way."

"That's alright, take a cab. I'll keep you paid."

"Okay," 1 replied with an ignorant mind.

So now look what i'm doing?

What is he doing
with all this humping and jumping?

I wish he'd hurry up and get off me.

I feel so dirty

and meek.
He didn't even tell me
he loved me.

What am I doing?

So this is what they call screwing.

I don't see what all the hype is about.

They're just

I Won't Apologize For Being a Woman SPECIAL EDITION
by Zorina Exie Jerome

in

and

they're

out.

I Won't Apologize For Being a Woman SPECIAL EDITION
by Zorina Exie Jerome

COMPROMISE

God has set me a little higher than the angels.

So, if I choose to love you,
will I be rejecting my Savior? I know God is love and love is God but, if I
believe to assume your plight, might I offend thee?

Please take the mote from my eye, for I can not see clearly.
You are near me
but all I want to do,

Is to have you.

Understand me. Tell me.
What the deal is.

Do I make you identify your true identity?
Am I an extension? Another entity?

Feel me.

You are near me.

Yet, you fear me.

I am taking the mote from your eye so you can see me clearly.

I Won't Apologize For Being a Woman SPECIAL EDITION
by Zorina Exie Jerome

My God

has set me a little higher than the angels.
So if I show you favor, will I be out of order? Further more,
results of compromise is devised in my mind.

Figuring our why? Figuring out what?
Figuring out why?
Figuring out what?

Figuring out why.

I want to give in, but my mouth speaks of things that seem impossible to achieve. My mind is set free. So free, it doesn't always make sense to me.

I'm in a position to accept what I see as though it is as good as it gets,
when the good…the good is unseen.

I Won't Apologize For Being a Woman SPECIAL EDITION
by Zorina Exie Jerome

DENIAL

Is it over?

This brief rendezvous between me and my lover?
I should've known, for this relationship was kept undercover.

Doomed from day one.

Never having the chance to blossom
because we never had the freedom to become what we wanted to become.

is it over?

I could've sworn I found a four-leaf clover.
Tainted with poison ivy.
Blinding me

to see
what reality holds
for you
and me?
Is it over?

I Won't Apologize For Being a Woman SPECIAL EDITION
by Zorina Exie Jerome

NOT HAVING IT

How many times must I be rejected?
How many times must I be bruised?

How many times must I be embarrassed?

This life of mine tries to re-enact the same nightmare.

See, that is implying the past to be brought to the present and that's sin so

I'm not trying to do that again.

Yet, the same play seems to go for show.

Different actors, different actresses you know?

I stand against this thing and persuade myself not to accept the same outcome.

At the same time, not drawing my own conclusions.

Rebuking the spirit of illusions.

YOU CAN LOVE AGAIN

If you cut yourself,
there's an immediate pain.
Blood running out.
Body being drained.
The wound is as deep as you let it get.
If it gets too deep,
you'll literally get sick.
Emotional and physical scars are one in the same.
The difference is,
with emotional ones,
you can control the pain.
Leave it up to the devil,
he'll drive you insane.
Ask Jesus for help
and he'll drive that demon of pain away so stay
prayerful.

Emotional and physical scars are one in the same.
Always remember,

you can love again.

I Won't Apologize For Being a Woman SPECIAL EDITION
by Zorina Exie Jerome

WRITE OFF

Listen man,

I begged and pleaded for you to listen to me,
but you weren't trying to hear it.

Know this;

As long as you keep your selfish ways,
there will come a day
when you will have to pay.

But I'm not trying to stick around

to see that day.

So as long as you keep those ugly ways,
I'm leaving.

Ghost.

To see much brighter and happier days.

I Won't Apologize For Being a Woman SPECIAL EDITION
by Zorina Exie Jerome

OH YES. SEXY DRESS!

Oh yes, I come dressed with a baby-T and tight jeans! Yes, I realize these pants accentuate my ass! As a matter of fact, I'm quite conscience of this chest. Oh yes, you're looking at a bonafide woman. God's creation. Baby-making, heart aching, warrior-praying, head-held-up-high-portraying a strong woman. Oh yes, I am woman! Why should I be ashamed of that which makes me feminine when dudes can beat their chest and sweat like He-Man and I'm supposed to pretend that doesn't phase me?

I prefer a successful man with more than just…something in his pants. More like being rich in the spiritual. Common sense in the mental. Not afraid to spend when it's time to spend some time. Can control himself around this. Patient because he knows eventually, he'll get this because he's handling his business and he knows not too many men are doing this! He recognizes a real Miss and he's not stupid enough to let this sift through his strong hands. Oh yes! I've got a man! Lazy ones can't understand how come they weren't capable of handling it.

Let me scream, "On your knees please!" Open your mouth and take these words. Don't chew, just swallow and let these words follow through. Flush out what you don't need and what stops you from being free.

I Won't Apologize For Being a Woman SPECIAL EDITION
by Zorina Exie Jerome

Oh yes, I came dressed like this. Those who lack self-control, get pissed. Wish they could get this, but they chose the quick and easy—shhh! That's why their pissed. I flaunt my body with class. Even if I wear baggy pants, you'd still be thinking 'bout my ass and the next one! I'm not dumb. One way or another, you'll get some! Even if it isn't me it might be the weak one who uses your stick as a scepter. Please reference my poem called, "A Letter".

Oh yes I'm snapping. Informing and happening. Don't get it twisted. This is not a green light to start twisting dressing like you're in the red light district. Ladies, you missed it. If you can't do it with class, then sit your ass down! Don't even bother. Probably just want your father. Confused classy with nasty. Access your figure or get tossed up by a no-good trickster numerating any nationality.

As for me? Oh yes. I'm free.

CORDIAL

To flow poetically is as easy as 1-2-3.

I'm telling you, it's from The Good Book I feed. Let's be cordial and get cordial like a stimulating medicine or drink. You might say,

"Please."

The question I have for you is how do you like your coffee?

Let's use the analogy of the coffeepot. God is the water. Our hearts are the filter. Our mouths are the spouts.

Do you know what I'm talking about?

God's Spirit is the living water percolating in our body. The heart is the filter where the living water runs through to deliver. Our heart will determine just how pure our words will be. Will it run though freely or get contaminated by the cares of this world?

Would you drink the water of envy, vainglory or strife?

The living water of Christ I desire to testify. Instead of obeying my thirst, I desire to obey His word, according to the grace He has set in me.

Um-um-um, I love this type of coffee!

I Won't Apologize For Being a Woman SPECIAL EDITION
by Zorina Exie Jerome

Excuse me but may I have some cream with that? Yes, and a little bit of milk to go down smoothly? Blend it with some ice and it'll stick like a smoothie. Get the picture? Like a movie? I'm talking of the living water running through me. Something like coffee.

Either hot or cold, the beauty of The Lord, I will behold.

The heart is desperately deceitful. Who can know it? The living waters will test and try it. The fruit will come out the mouth. No need to try and hide it.

The ministry of The Christ comes out, I can't fight it.

So if you desire a stronger drink, don't be a fiend. The question for you is,

How do you like your coffee?

Say you're looking for a stimulating drink. Coffee, per-say. So stimulating, you might buy the whole shop. But, before you invest your stock you try the café shops out.

You know fellas, to see what the girl's all about?

The problem is, some men are shrewd businessmen. Nasty and conniving. Acting as an angel in disguise, hoarding the virtue of other women, which was stolen.

Her heart, you left broken because unto you, she opened. Trying to act as her savior. You wanted her to pursue you first, rather than The Savior. When she finally did, toward her you

I Won't Apologize For Being a Woman SPECIAL EDITION
by Zorina Exie Jerome

became disgusted. Dropped her and kicked her quick. Like a bucket. Exposed by light. Now who's the sucker?

The one who repents from their mistakes or the one who keeps raising the stakes? Continually give thanks. I love you but what you're doing my brother just isn't cool.

I suppose there's nothing wrong with investing. How else will you determine the quality in your coffee? However, if she's not your cup of tea, move on and leave that Coca-Cola bottle alone. She may not be the right one. If she has a baby, are you ready to take on the role as a daddy? Or are you just slapping the mammy? Let God's joy make you happy. I love you but what you're doing my brother just isn't cool.

Dude, don't you realize you're witnessing soulless nations dying of madness and insanity from irrationality. Yet, you choose to close your eyes and deny.

The lack of depth in your eyes explains why you won't look yourself in the eye.

Only at the man-made atonement thinking you've got it going on.

Whatever.

No one can tell you anything. I love you but, you're not cool.

You can go visit various coffee shops if you want but don't drink from just anybody's spout. Do you know what I'm

I Won't Apologize For Being a Woman SPECIAL EDITION
by Zorina Exie Jerome

talking about? If you go around doing the taste test here and there, you won't be able to identify the real thing when it's time to share.

For your tongue will be numb from too much honey from the comb.

Too much honey and you'll eventually vomit.

My brothers, take heed.

You just might be drinking from the woman who sits on the seven-headed beast.

Don't believe me? Read Revelations 17.

Yeah dude, you might be drinking from The Great Prostitute who sits on many waters.

But keep your head up because Christ is in the strongest muscle in our vessel. So continue to wet your whistle to trample the subtle with the living water.

Your mate may be black, sweet, might be mixed with Irish cream. Might be spiced with a bit of Amaretto. This flow can go on and on like sap from a tree planted by the flowing agua.

The sappy water sticks like syrup so sip that with your coffee. Anything less is skimmed and frothy. The question still remains;

How do you like your coffee?

I Won't Apologize For Being a Woman SPECIAL EDITION
by Zorina Exie Jerome

God is the water. Our hearts are the filter. Our mouths are the spout. Do you know what I'm talking about?

To flow poetically is as easy as 1-2-3. I'm telling you, it's from The Good Book I feed. You might say,

"Whatever. Please."

Let's be cordial and get cordial like a stimulating medicine or drink.

Um-um-um!

I like this type of coffee!

The Merriam
Webster Dictionary

cor-dial adj : warmly receptive or welcoming.
cordial n : a stimulating medicine or drink.

I Won't Apologize For Being a Woman SPECIAL EDITION
by Zorina Exie Jerome

WHAT'S HER PURPOSE?

Almost every woman claims she wants a real man, right?

Yet when one comes along, her first mission is to change him. To break him. To make him a Mrs. instead of the Mister God made him to be all because we sought man first and our purpose as a woman last. Our mission we think, is to conquer and divide the man. Confuse him. Less he understands. This is contrary to God's plan.

See, we need to be careful not to break and shape the man as if we're the ones with the plan. It is known Jehovah made man so, why can't we just let a man be a man?

Why?

Because it hurts to deny ourselves. Well, welcome to another episode of longsuffering.

Love is a painful thing to maintain.

Godly love that is.

Constantly sacrificing...

God help us.

Ladies, we need to seek our own purpose.

God is the artist. It is His job to break and shape but, that spirit of Jezebel wants to get in the way with no shame.

I Won't Apologize For Being a Woman SPECIAL EDITION
by Zorina Exie Jerome

This thing is exposed! The door is closed! Manipulative whores can be no more.

See, a whore is more than just sex without the wedding ring. You are tripping if you think you can take the reigns because that's not you're thing.

To manipulate him so he can grant your every wish. Using a tool talking about what you can dish? Or not.

Girlfriend, you know you need to stop!

Don't pretend like that wasn't your plan.

It's in the light now. No more manipulating the man.

Let the man be a man.

So now you have a glimpse of your purpose, not your destiny. Although you know it's to reign with Christ, there are still some things you have yet to see.

For if all women knew their purpose or at least sought to seek it then, maybe this would encourage man to improve before he made his move but we seem to make it easy and run to them instead of Jesus.

Ladies, we are quite unaware of the power God has invested in us.

Maybe not.

Because some whores sure know how to go for theirs what is not.

I Won't Apologize For Being a Woman SPECIAL EDITION
by Zorina Exie Jerome

Girlfriend, you know you need to stop!

I hope for the guilty, these words pierce your hearts. Then maybe you'll just stop and be spared of the consequences. Those with hardened hearts will only do it again. Guaranteed one day to cry,

"Lord forgive me, for I have sinned!"

But the true children of God will love you anyway because it wasn't long ago when I had my day! So keep reading God's word. It'll be OK.

I say all this to say,

Let the man be a man in Christ because that is all part of God's plan.

I Won't Apologize For Being a Woman SPECIAL EDITION
by Zorina Exie Jerome

IT'S A WEAVE, GET OVER IT!

Weave. Wig. Tracks. Whatever! It's a weave, get over it! What's the big deal, anyway? Why the fascination? Why do you feel the need to ask whether or not my hair is my own? What satisfaction does that give you? Do you secretly feel relieved to know my hair is weaved in? Do you sigh inside because my own hair cannot possibly look this good? Does it give you a sense of superiority to degrade and dissect me?

What?

Do you gather together in a private conference discussing why my hair is short one day and long the next? It's a weave, get over it!

I swear it feels like challenge at the O.K. Corral—"Is that your hair?" She asks me supported by a handful of curious-eyed women; all who seemed seem to have sucked the air out of the room waiting for a response to a question they already know the answer to.

I swear, I didn't know you cared so much! I didn't know you spent such a great deal of thought about what is on my head because I never gave it much thought to why her teeth were so straight and why her gums are as pink as Salt-Water Taffy. Could they be dentures? She had a pot belly and rolls yesterday and unusually flat and smooth today. Girdle? Laugh lines today, giddy cheesy teenager tomorrow! Collagen? "A" cup this week. "D" cup the next! Wonderbra? Waterbra? Silicon?

I Won't Apologize For Being a Woman SPECIAL EDITION
by Zorina Exie Jerome

Maybe, I'll ask a few nosey women who have nothing else to discuss but whether or not the adornment on another woman is natural or enhanced and ask them why, at the most unusual time, say in the break room where there's an audience they pounce on the poor girl, striking the appalling question:

"Are those real?"

Yes, it's tacky. It's rude. It's really none of your business.

It's a weave! Get over it!

I'm not done yet.

To my sisters who believe wearing a weave denounces my ethnicity, who believe I do not love myself because I prefer chemicals over an afro and braids over dred-locs, who believe I am trying to be somebody I'm not because I've experimented with different eye colors, I say to you with all due respect: I am beautiful when I wake up. I am beautiful before I go to bed. I am beautiful with an afro. I am beautiful with dred-locs, long hair, straight hair, curly hair, or braided hair. I am sexy wearing a girdle. I am curvy without it. I am alluring with my brown eyes. I dazzle with hazel eyes. I am a supermodel with a minimizer. I am voluptuous supermodel with a padded bra. I am elegant with acrylics. I am simply charming with my own bed of nails. I am an artist. I love the way I look, which is why I choose to model any style I wish and look simply ravishing in all of them. And I know it! At the end of the day, I can strip everything off and still like what I see. It's still me. I know who I am.

I Won't Apologize For Being a Woman SPECIAL EDITION
by Zorina Exie Jerome

I am a beautiful.

I am sexy.

I am diverse.

I am a woman.

It is a weave.

Get over it!

BONUS CHAPTER

From the next book

How to Conquer Haters
By
Zorina Exie Jerome

Coming Soon!

2011

www.iwa.yolasite.com

I Won't Apologize For Being a Woman SPECIAL EDITION
by Zorina Exie Jerome

Chapter 1: WHAT IS A HATER?

I am not a doctor and I do not claim to have all of the answers as to how one should cope with negativity. However, I can only tell you what works for the impartial. Conquering the negativity in your life is a fight, but it is not a physical one. It is a state of mind. How do you deal with the negativity in your life? Should you tell the person who has offended you about themselves immediately? Should you let the whole situation role off your back? Should you treat them the same way they treat you? Do you tell on them? Do you seek revenge? What do you do?

Well, an impartial person will not tell you exactly what to do because every situation in life requires a unique way of dealing with it. This all depends on the type of personality involved in such conflicting situations. In reference to the book *I Won't Apologize For Being A Woman*, like the character Hate is to Jealousy, Envy, and Slander, Haters have different characteristics. Here is a list of some of them:

- *The Phony Friend.*

These people are opportunist. They are indeed very good friends and are usually there for you in a time of need. They might even display sincere compassion. However, if an opportunity to better themselves or associate with a more favorable crowd emerges, they will not do it on their own merit; they will use you as a dirty tool to get it.

Have you ever had a friend who acted a completely different way once you got around other people? Have you ever had your trust betrayed? Have you encountered a person who blabbed to you the dirty secrets of people whom you did not know? Do you catch them in several meaningless white lies? If this person lies about little things, you better believe the bigger lies are right around the corner. It is only a matter of time before you are weaved into the next web of lies.

- *The Spoiled Rotten Person.*

    These people have lived sheltered lives and either are not aware or do not care about other societies and cultures outside of their own. They take confidence in understanding different races and cultures by believing what is fed to them through the media. They lack diversity and are typically tolerant of other races and cultures and suffer a severe case of ethnocentrism.

I Won't Apologize For Being a Woman SPECIAL EDITION
by Zorina Exie Jerome

Their compassion for the poor and needy is almost non-existent. Their way of thinking is usually one-sided, meaning their way is right and everyone else is wrong.

- *The Material Person.*

    This is the person who loves keeping up with the Joneses. They take enjoying the finer things in life to another level by defining their self-worth with material things they possess. They are competitors and are notorious for one-upping you. Just perform a little test. Women, buy a purse. Men, buy or lease a new car. The more compliments you get, the quicker this material person will try to top you with a new this or that to divert the attention toward them. These people may often take advantage of the latest gimmick and love to brag about it. Whether man or woman, they are catty and look down on people who do not have the luxuries of life.

- *The Gossiper.*

    They are often trouble-makers, liars, and will play the victim should their lies become exposed. They are incapable of holding a secret. The more drama they can create the more attention they believe they will have. They gain most of their information by becoming your friend, extracting your goals, fears, and aspirations. They glib about anything and nothing and they do it perpetually. They will not hesitate to exploit you and bring you into in their drama! They are also huge braggers. Basically, anything that will attract attention is up for grabs.

- *The Sanctified.*

    The sanctified may be the most disheartening type of Hater because they present themselves as devout and righteous. They are charismatic and talk AT you heavily referencing biblical scripture instead of TO you like a human being. They love for their good works to be seen and talked about and are always looking for a pet project (you) that they can exercise their so-called generous ways toward so people can see just how...nice they are. They have assumed because they go to church, they are better than someone who does not. They belittle people who they believe are not as religious as they are and are very condescending.

- *The Envious.*

    They have a very bitter personality and stew in hate. They show their envy through insults and sarcastic remarks. Their personality is nasty and bitingly vicious. They will put down everything about you that makes you shine. Their bark is certainly worse than their bite but their bark is something to be reckoned with. Their spiteful words are the very weapon they use to insult you. They find your weakness and use sarcasm to point it out. Sarcasm is basically an improper way to point out an ugly truth followed by the facetious excuse: *I'm just kidding!* In actuality, they really wish they could have everything you have and resent you for it.

- *The Belittler.*

    This is the classic school yard bully, the weakest Hater of them all. They pick on people. They gain popularity by humiliating others who appear to be an easy target. They provoke fear and look for easy prey to intimidate. Except the only people they will pick on are the weak and timid. Particularly, people who have not learned how to stand up for themselves and were probably victims of past offenses. The Belittler usually can sniff out victims of rejection and use that to their advantage.

- *The Copycat.*

    This is probably the most dangerous kind of Hater. They try to become someone who they are envious of by mirroring their personality. For example, they may try to adopt your clothing preference, sense of work practice, your hobbies, literally talk like you or recycle something you have said for their personal or professional gain. Once they have acquired enough of your personality, they will glib grandiloquence about themselves. They are usually loud, obnoxious, and charming towards the weak. Beware of this type of personality. Before you know it, you may be dealing with an evil twin version of yourself!

- *The Whore.*

    The Whore defines themselves and their worth by their significant other(s). They have no regard or respect for relationships or marriage. They cannot function without a partner and are incapable of being independent. Once they do grab a partner they will obsess over other people's relationships. This is usually because they are not happy in their own. As a result, they work on making other relationships as miserable or even worse than their own in order to make their lives seem better. Married or single, they are shamelessly flirtatious and may inveigle their so-called friendliness as having Tom-Boy attributes or in the man's case, being...sensitive. Beware. They may not try to take your place but they will certainly find out if they can and make sure you know it.

Out of all of these characteristics, you will find that they can also be intertwined with one another. Depending on an individual's cultural and social background, there could be thousands upon thousands of personality combinations. It is up to you to determine which one of these traits you are dealing with and engage it accordingly. These personalities are similar to Jerome's poem, *Awaken* where the characters Envy, Jealously, and Slander morph into one big snake called "Hate" (p.27 original verion and p.31 *Special Edition*). Likewise, The Phony Friend, The Spoiled Rotten Person, The Material Person, The Gossiper, The Sanctified, The Envious, The Belittler, The Copycat, and The Whore are all Haters!

Haters can be anywhere. They may be a friend, an enemy, family, or dare I say clergy? You will encounter them in your schools, place of employment, your home, the grocery store, gas station, and almost in any organization or institution and yes, even in church! You may be led to believe that you are somehow insufficient and they reign supreme in all that they do when actually, it is quite the opposite.

How to Conquer Haters

By
Zorina Exie Jerome

Coming Soon!

2011

www.iwa.yolasite.com

I Won't Apologize For Being a Woman SPECIAL EDITION
by Zorina Exie Jerome

Purchase

I.W.A.

I WON'T APOLOGIZE!

Clothing and Accessories

at

http://www.cafepress.com/IWONTAPOLOGIZE

Made in the USA
Charleston, SC
22 January 2011